Cool
FRUIT & VEGGIE FOOD ART

Easy Recipes That Make Food Fun to Eat!

Nancy Tuminelly

ABDO
Publishing Company

Visit us at www.abdopublishing.com

Published by ABDO Publishing Company, 8000 West 78th Street, Edina, Minnesota 55439. Copyright © 2011 by Abdo Consulting Group, Inc. International copyrights reserved in all countries. No part of this book may be reproduced in any form without written permission from the publisher. Checkerboard Library™ is a trademark and logo of ABDO Publishing Company.

Printed in the United States of America, North Mankato, Minnesota
062010
092010

 PRINTED ON RECYCLED PAPER

Editor: Liz Salzmann
Series Concept: Nancy Tuminelly
Cover and Interior Design: Anders Hanson, Mighty Media, Inc.
Photo Credits: Anders Hanson, Shutterstock

The following manufacturers/names appearing in this book are trademarks:
The Laughing Cow®, T. Marzetti™, Wilton®

Library of Congress Cataloging-in-Publication Data

Tuminelly, Nancy, 1952-
Cool fruit & veggie food art : easy recipes that make food fun to eat! / Nancy Tuminelly.
  p. cm. -- (Cool food art)
Includes index.
ISBN 978-1-61613-364-1
1. Cookery--Juvenile literature. I. Title.
TX652.5.T84 2010
641.58--dc22

2010003285

To Adult Helpers

This is not your ordinary cookbook! Sure, we've provided ingredients lists and how-to photographs. But like any artistic endeavor, food art is all about creativity! Encourage kids to come up with their own ideas. Get creative with ingredients too. Scan your fridge and get started with whatever you have!

Always supervise kids when they are working in the kitchen. Food art often requires a lot of knife work such as slicing and shaping. Assist young artists whenever they are using knives. Occasionally, kids will need to use the oven or stovetop too. Be there to help when necessary, but encourage them to do as much as they can on their own. Kids love to share and eat their own creations!

Expect your young food artists to make a mess, but also expect them to clean up after themselves. Show them how to properly store unused ingredients. Most importantly, be a voice of encouragement. You might even get kids to eat healthy foods they've never had before!

CONTENTS

PLAY WITH YOUR FOOD!

Unless mom says not to!

It's time to play with your food! Get ready to make faces, animals, and bugs! You're an artist now. The plate is your **canvas**, and your favorite foods are your paints!

As you make your fruit and veggie food art, be open to all sorts of ingredients. You can use anything! Fresh fruits and vegetables work great. You can shape and slice them in so many ways! Use foods that you like, but don't be afraid to try new things.

Like any kind of art, food art is about **expression** and creativity. Get inspired and give each dish your own special touch. A lot of cookbooks teach you how to make food that tastes great. This book will inspire you to make fruit and veggie that tastes and looks great!

THE BASICS

Get started with a few important basics

ASK PERMISSION

➤ Before you cook, get permission to use the kitchen, cooking tools, and ingredients.

➤ You might want an adult to help you with some of your creations. But if you want to do something yourself, say so!

➤ When you need help, just ask. An adult should always be around when you are using sharp knives, the oven, or the stove.

BE PREPARED

➤ Read through the recipe before you begin.

➤ Get organized. Have your tools and ingredients ready before you start.

➤ Think of **alternative** ingredients if you want!

BE SMART, BE SAFE

‣ Never work in the kitchen when you are home alone!

‣ Have an adult nearby when you are using sharp tools such as a knife, peeler, or grater. Always use sharp tools with care. Use a cutting board when you are working with a knife.

‣ Work slowly and carefully. Great food art rarely happens when you rush!

BE NEAT AND CLEAN

‣ Start with clean hands, clean tools, and a clean work surface.

‣ Always wash fruits and vegetables. Rinse them under cold water. Pat them dry with a towel. Then they won't slip when you cut them.

‣ Tie back long hair so it stays out of the way and out of the food!

‣ Wear comfortable clothes that can get a little bit dirty. Roll up your sleeves.

Note on Measuring

The recipes in this book provide **approximations**. Feel free to be creative! For example, a recipe may call for 1 tablespoon of cream cheese. Do you like cream cheese? Then add more! If you don't like cream cheese, then try something else!

SHOPPING FOR PRODUCE

Sometimes canned produce works perfectly in your food art. But more often than not, fresh fruits and vegetables are better. When you are shopping for your food art groceries, think about what you are making. For example, do you want a really big cucumber or a small one? Fruits and vegetables come in all different shapes and sizes! Think about the shapes and sizes that will work best in your food art.

SAVING INGREDIENTS

When you are making food art, sometimes you only need a little bit of something. That means you have to do a good job of putting things away so they stay fresh. Cover leftover ingredients so that they will keep. Airtight containers work best. You don't want to waste a lot of food!

KEY SYMBOLS

In this book, you may see a symbol beside the recipes. Here is what it means.

Sharp!

You need to use a knife for this recipe. Ask an adult to stand by.

CUCUMBERS

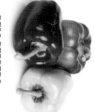

BELL PEPPERS

LETTUCE HEAD

SLICED TURKEY

BABY CARROTS

MUSHROOMS

MIXED LETTUCE

HARD-BOILED EGG

CARROTS

GREEN ONIONS

ONION

CHEESE WEDGE

8

SUNFLOWER SEEDS

BROCCOLI

BLACK OLIVES

CREAM CHEESE

SLICED ALMONDS

CELERY

CAULIFLOWER HEAD

FETA CHEESE

RADISHES

VEGGIE DIP

THE COOLEST

INGREDIENTS

BLACK ICING

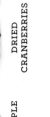

CANTALOUPE

RAISINS

TOMATO

CARAMEL DIP

HONEYDEW MELON

DRIED CRANBERRIES

GRAPE TOMATOES

MINI MARSHMALLOWS

LEMONS

GREEN APPLE

GREEN BEANS

MARSHMALLOWS

RED GRAPES

LIMA BEANS

PULL AND PEEL LICORICE

MANDARIN ORANGE

GREEN GRAPES

SUGAR SNAP PEAS

FRUIT LEATHER ROLL

STRAWBERRIES

SMALL WATERMELON

GREEN PEAS

9

THE TOOL BOX

Here are some tools you'll need for most food art recipes

LARGE KNIFE

PARING KNIFE

APPLE CORER

MELON BALL SCOOP

MEASURING CUPS AND SPOONS

PASTRY ICING TIP

WOODEN SKEWERS

TOOTHPICKS

MIXING BOWLS

VEGETABLE PEELER

CUTTING BOARD

COOKING TERMS

A simple list of words you'll want to know

CHOPPING

Chop means to cut things into small pieces. The more you chop, the smaller the pieces. If a recipe says finely chopped, it means you need very small pieces.

SLICING

Slice means to cut something into thin pieces. Each slice should be about the same thickness.

CUTTING LENGTHWISE

To cut something lengthwise means to cut *along* its length. You create pieces that are the *same length* as they were initially.

CUTTING CROSSWISE

To cut something crosswise means to cut *across* its length. The pieces will be shorter, but the *same width* as they were initially.

11

TECHNIQUES

Tips for making great food art

MAKING FACES

Food art is all about creativity. The recipes in this book will get you started. But your imagination is really the secret ingredient! A recipe may call for black olives as the eyes. But why not try raisins instead? Use these techniques for inspiration. Add your personal style to create cool variations!

Eyes

GRAPE HALVES ON MARSHMALLOWS

BLACK OLIVE SLICES ON CREAM CHEESE

BLUEBERRIES ON BANANA SLICES

BLACK OLIVES ON HARD-BOILED EGGS

Noses

CANTALOUPE BALL

BABY CARROT

RAISIN

GRAPE TOMATO

Mouths

HALF A LEMON SLICE

RED PEPPER TOP

ORANGE SECTION

GREEN PEPPER SLICE

12

ATTACHING WITH GOOEY STUFF

Food art combines a variety of ingredients. How do you hold them all together? Ingredients such as peanut butter, mayonnaise, and cream cheese can be used like glue. Plus, they taste great!

ATTACHING WITH TOOTHPICKS

When you're making food art, it's a good idea to keep toothpicks handy. You can use them in so many ways! They are great for making small holes in ingredients. Plus, you can use them to hold ingredients together! Just be careful not to bite into them!

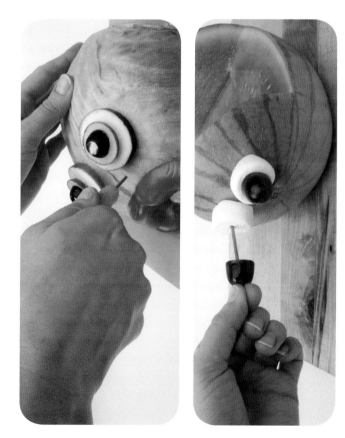

FABULOUS FROGGY

Look who hopped onto your plate!

1 Cut the apple into quarters. Cut the core off of the back of each piece.

2 Cut a thin wedge lengthwise out of one of the apple pieces. Set the piece of apple on its side.

3 To make the eyes, cut a raisin in half. Push each half into the side of a mini marshmallow. Use cream cheese to **attach** the eyes to the top of the apple.

4 To make the front legs, cut a green grape in half lengthwise. Use a little cream cheese to stick one half on each side of the frog.

5 To make the feet, cut a green grape in half lengthwise. Then cut each half in half crosswise. Cut little wedges out of the rounded side of each piece of grape to make toes. Move the frog to a plate. Set two of the feet against the bottoms of the front legs. Set the other two feet against the front of the frog.

6 Cut off a piece of fruit leather that is about 1 x 3 inches (3 x 8 cm). Round off the corners of one end. Put the other end in the frog's mouth. Stick two almond slices into a raisin to make a fly. Set the fly on the frog's tongue.

MAKES 4 FROGS

INGREDIENTS

1 green apple

8 raisins

8 mini marshmallows

1 tablespoon cream cheese

8 green grapes

1 fruit leather roll

8 almond slices

TOOLS

cutting board

paring knife

15

MICE
MOUTHFULS

These little mice are bite-size perfection!

INGREDIENTS

1 large strawberry

4-inch strip of pull and peel licorice

1 raisin

black icing

2 almond slices

small wedge of cheese

TOOLS

paring knife

cutting board

toothpick

pastry icing tip

1 Cut the leaf off of the strawberry. Cut a small slice off the bottom so it will sit flat.

2 Use a toothpick to make a small hole in the back of the strawberry. Push the end of the licorice into the hole. This is the mouse's tail.

3 Press a raisin into the tip of the strawberry for the nose. Add small dots of black icing for the eyes. Push two almond slices into the top to make ears.

4 Serve with a little triangle of cheese.

GRAPE MICE

Fresh out of strawberries? Try this recipe with grapes instead!

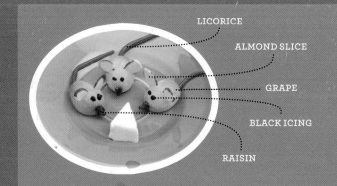

LICORICE

ALMOND SLICE

GRAPE

BLACK ICING

RAISIN

FUNNY FACE
SALAD

This is the silliest salad you'll ever meet!

INGREDIENTS

2 handfuls of
mixed lettuce

4 slices of turkey

1 hard-boiled egg,
peeled

1 black olive

1 grape tomato

1 carrot

1 mushroom,
whole

1 red bell pepper

2 green onions

TOOLS

paring knife

cutting board

1 Place two handfuls of lettuce on a plate.

2 Cut the turkey into strips. Arrange it around the lettuce as hair.

3 Cut the hard-boiled egg in half. Set the halves yolk side up on the lettuce. Put a slice of olive on each yolk.

4 Place a grape tomato in the center of the salad for a nose.

5 Cut a carrot in half crosswise. Cut each half lengthwise into three strips. To make a bow tie, arrange the carrot strips on each side of the mushroom top.

6 Cut a thin slice of red pepper for the mouth.

7 Cut the bottom off the red pepper. Slice it in half. Set it on the salad as a hat. Cut off the tops of the green onions. Stick them under the hat to look like tassels.

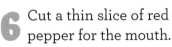

19

APPLE
FLUTTERFLY

Don't let it fly off your plate!

INGREDIENTS

8 tablespoons caramel dip

4 baby carrots

1 green apple

1 celery stalk

dried cranberries and sunflower seeds (optional)

TOOLS

paring knife

cutting board

toothpick

1 Put 2 tablespoons of caramel dip in center of a plate. Shape it so it is about the same size as a baby carrot.

2 Place a baby carrot on top of the caramel.

3 Cut the apple into quarters. Cut the core off the back of each piece. Cut each piece into seven slices. Cut four of the slices in half.

4 Arrange three apple slices on each side of the carrot. Put two half slices at the bottom.

5 Cut the celery into eight strips. Place two strips at the top of the flutterfly for antennae. Decorate the wings with cranberries and sunflower seeds.

PEAR FLUTTERFLY

Fresh out of apples? Try it with a pear instead. It's bursting with flavor!

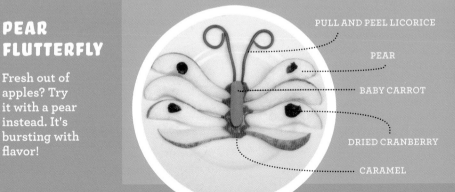

PULL AND PEEL LICORICE

PEAR

BABY CARROT

DRIED CRANBERRY

CARAMEL

CATNIP AND DIP

This cat is cool, no bones about it!

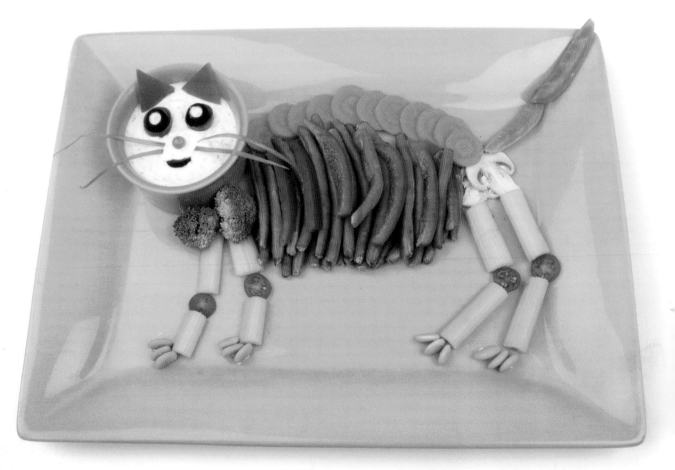

INGREDIENTS

1 carrot, sliced

20 to 25 green beans

1 red bell pepper

2 broccoli florets

1 mushroom

1 celery stalk

2 grape tomatoes

12 lima beans

cream cheese

2 sugar snap peas

1 container vegetable dip

2 black olives

1 green pea

1 green onion

TOOLS

cutting board

paring knife

1 Select a large **platter** as the background. Find a small bowl that is a good size for the cat's face. Set the bowl on the platter.

2 Arrange carrot slices in a row for the spine. Pile the green beans below the spine for the body. Add red pepper slices for stripes.

3 Use the broccoli florets for the cat's neck area. Use mushroom slices for the tops of the back legs.

4 Make the legs with celery sticks and the knees out of grape tomato slices. Arrange lima beans for the feet. Use a bit of cream cheese to stick them to the platter. Add two sugar snap peas for the tail.

5 Fill the bowl with vegetable dip and make the surface smooth. Make the eyes out of slices of grape tomato and black olive. Put a little vegetable dip in the center of the black olive slices.

6 Use a small slice of black olive for the mouth. Use a pea for the nose. Make whiskers out of green onion tops sliced very thin. Cut triangles out of red pepper for the ears.

WATERMELON
MOBILE

Now you can haul your favorite fruits anywhere!

INGREDIENTS

1 small watermelon

1 marshmallow

1 red grape

1 lemon

10 Mandarin orange slices

10 balls cantaloupe

10 balls honeydew melon

10 green grapes

TOOLS

cutting board

large knife

paring knife

toothpicks

melon ball scoop

mixing bowl

1 Slice a thin piece off the bottom of the watermelon so it won't roll around. Cut the top half off, leaving about 2 inches (5 cm) on each end. Cut the piece you removed into cubes.

2 Cut the marshmallow in half. Press the sticky side of each half onto the front of the watermelon for eyes. Cut the red grape in half. Stick each half onto a marshmallow with a toothpick.

3 Cut five slices of lemon. Use toothpicks to stick four of them to the watermelon for wheels. Cut the remaining slice in half. Use a toothpick to stick one half onto the watermelon for the mouth.

4 Stick a Mandarin orange slice over each eye for eyebrows.

5 Scoop about ten melon balls out of a cantaloupe. Then scoop about ten melon balls out of a honeydew melon. Use one cantaloupe ball as the nose. **Attach** it with a toothpick.

6 In a bowl, mix the watermelon cubes, mandarin orange slices, melon balls, and green grapes together. Gently pile the fruit into the open space in the watermelon.

25

VEG HEAD

PARTY PLEASER

This veggie head will blow your mind!

INGREDIENTS

1 head iceberg
lettuce

8 bell peppers,
any color

1 cucumber

1 bunch radishes

vegetable dip

6-ounce can
black olives

2 carrots

13 mushrooms

6 green beans

1 pint grape
tomatoes

1 broccoli crown

1 cauliflower head

TOOLS

paring knife

cutting board

toothpicks

wooden skewers

1 Rinse the iceberg lettuce. Remove the core. Set the lettuce core side down on a **platter**. This is the head.

2 Slice the top off of a bell pepper. Lay the top on a cutting board and cut out the center. This is the mouth. Use toothpicks to **attach** it to the head.

3 Make the eyes. Put a slice of radish on top of a slice of cucumber. Attach the eye to the head with a toothpick. Slice the top off of a black olive. Use vegetable dip to attach it to the center of the eye. Make the second eye the same way.

4 Cut the tip off of a carrot for the nose. Use a toothpick to attach it to the head.

5 Slice the tops off of two of the bell peppers. Wash the peppers and remove the seeds. Set the peppers next to the head for the ears.

6 Use toothpicks to attach the green beans over the eyes for eyebrows. Put a few mushrooms around the bottom of the head.

7 Wash the rest of the vegetables. Cut the large ones into small pieces. Put the vegetables on wooden skewers. Make about 8 skewers. Stick the skewers into the lettuce head. Fill the "ears" with vegetable dip.

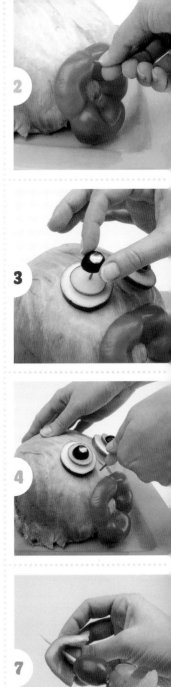

FLYING
CUCUMBER

Get your cucumber prepared for takeoff!

INGREDIENTS

1 cucumber

¼ cup tomato, chopped

½ cup mixed lettuce

¼ cup feta cheese

2 tablespoons onion, chopped

2 tablespoons sunflower seeds

1 carrot

1 black olive

cream cheese

TOOLS

measuring cups & spoons

cutting board

paring knife

melon ball scoop

apple corer

mixing bowl

vegetable peeler

1 Cut away a large section of the top of the cucumber. Use the melon ball scoop to scrape out the insides of both pieces of cucumber.

2 Use the apple corer to cut four holes on each side of the top cucumber piece.

3 Put the chopped tomato, mixed lettuce, feta cheese, chopped onion, and sunflower seeds into a bowl. Mix gently. Pile the mixture into the bottom cucumber piece.

4 Peel the carrot. Slice it lengthwise. You'll need three slices. Make each slice about ⅛ inch thick. You may need an adult helper for this step.

5 Cut a **slit** on each side of the bottom cucumber. **Insert** a carrot slice into each slit for the wings. Cut the third carrot slice into three smaller pieces for the tail. Cut three slits into the back for the tail pieces. Insert the carrot slices into the slits.

6 Use two sunflower seeds for eyes. Cut the black olive in half for the nose. **Attach** them to the front of the airplane with cream cheese.

WRAP IT UP!

Food art finale!

Now you're ready to **design** your own fruit and veggie food art! It helps to have a plan before you start. Make a **sketch** of your idea. Add notes about what ingredients might work best. Talk about your sketch with others. You will get great ideas! Make sure you take photographs before you eat your creations. The better your fruit and veggie food art looks, the more likely it is to be eaten!

It's good to learn about food. The foods we eat have a lot to do with how we feel. The more familiar you are with the food around you, the better! Learning to cook teaches us about **nutrition** and health. Learning to make food art teaches us to have fun at the same time!

GLOSSARY

ALTERNATIVE – different from the original.

APPROXIMATION – about the right amount.

ATTACH – to join two things together.

CANVAS – a type of thick cloth that artists paint on.

DESIGN – to plan how something will appear or work.

EXPRESSION – creating a work of art as a way to show one's feelings.

INSERT – to stick something into something else.

NUTRITION – how different foods affect one's health.

PLATTER – a large serving plate.

SKETCH – a drawing.

SLIT – a narrow cut or opening.

Web Sites

To learn more about cool food art, visit ABDO Publishing Company on the World Wide Web at **www.abdopublishing.com.** Web sites about cool food art are featured on our Book Links page. These links are routinely monitored and updated to provide the most current information available.

INDEX